◤SCHOLASTIC

National Curriculum
MATHS
Revision Guide

- ✓ Recap
- ✓ Revise
- ✓ Skills Check

Ages 6-7
Year 2

KS1

SCHOLASTIC

National Curriculum
MATHS
Revision Guide

Book End, Range Road, Witney, Oxfordshire, OX29 0YD
Registered office: Westfield Road, Southam, Warwickshire CV47 0RA
www.scholastic.co.uk

© 2016, Scholastic Ltd

5 6 7 8 9 8 9 0 1 2 3 4 5

British Library Cataloguing-in-Publication Data
A catalogue record for this book is available from the British Library.

ISBN 978-1407-15986-7
Printed in Malaysia

All rights reserved. This book is sold subject to the condition that it shall not, by way of trade or otherwise, be lent, hired out or otherwise circulated without the publisher's prior consent in any form of binding or cover other than that in which it is published and without a similar condition, including this condition, being imposed upon the subsequent purchaser.

No part of this publication may be reproduced, stored in a retrieval system, or transmitted, in any form or by any means, electronic, mechanical, photocopying, recording or otherwise, other than for the purposes described in the content of this product, without the prior permission of the publisher. This product remains in copyright.

Due to the nature of the web we cannot guarantee the content or links of any site mentioned. We strongly recommend that teachers check websites before using them in the classroom.

Every effort has been made to trace copyright holders for the works reproduced in this book, and the publishers apologise for any inadvertent omissions.

Author
Ann Montague-Smith

Consultant
Paul Hollin

Editorial
Rachel Morgan, Jenny Wilcox, Mark Walker, Mary Nathan, Margaret Eaton, Kate Baxter, Janette Ratcliffe and Julia Roberts

Series Design
Scholastic Design Team: Nicolle Thomas and Neil Salt

Design
Oxford Designers & Illustrators

Cover Design
Scholastic Design Team: Nicolle Thomas and Neil Salt

Cover Illustration
Shutterstock / © VIGE.CO

Illustration
Tom Heard, The Bright Agency

Contents

How to use this book 5

Revision tracker 7

Number and place value

Counting in steps 8

Reading and writing numbers to at
least 100 10

Comparing and ordering numbers 12

Recognising place value in 2-digit numbers .14

Showing numbers in different ways.............16

Using place value and number facts to
solve problems 18

Addition and subtraction

Addition and subtraction facts to 20 and related
facts to 100 20

Adding and subtracting mentally.................22

Adding and subtracting by using objects and
representations...............................24

Adding three 1-digit numbers 26

Checking calculations and missing
number problems 28

Solving problems with addition and
subtraction 30

Multiplication and division

Multiplication and division facts for the
10-times table 32

Multiplication and division facts for the
2- and 5-times tables 34

Odd and even numbers...............................36

Solving problems involving multiplication
and division 38

Adding numbers in any order 40

Multiplying numbers in any order 41

Fractions

Fractions of shapes 42

Finding fractions of numbers and
quantities....................................44

Recognising that $\frac{2}{4}$ is equivalent to $\frac{1}{2}$ 46

Measurement

Comparing and ordering measurements.......48

Choosing and using standard units..............50

Telling the time..................................52

Comparing and sequencing time 54

Money 56

Solving money problems 58

Geometry

Comparing and sorting 2D shapes 60

Comparing and sorting 3D shapes 62

Recognising 2D shapes on the surface
of 3D shapes 64

Patterns and sequences.............................66

Position, direction and movement................68

Statistics

Interpreting and making simple data charts...70

Using and making charts 72

Making totals and comparisons 73

Answers 74
Glossary 77
Multiplication table 80

How to use this book

Introduction

This book has been written to help children reinforce the mathematics they have learned at school. It provides information and varied examples, activities and questions in a clear and consistent format across 35 units, covering all of National Curriculum for Mathematics for this age group.

I give tips to children and adults alike!

Multiplication and division

Multiplication and division facts for the 2- and 5-times tables

↻ Recap

Here is the count in 2s.

0 2 4 6 8 10 12 14 16 18 20 22 24

This count in 2s is used in the 2-times table.

And here is the count in 5s.

0 5 10 15 20 25 30 35 40 45 50 55 60

This count in 5s is used in the 5-times table.

📝 Revise

2-times table	5-times table
1 × 2 = 2	1 × 5 = 5
2 × 2 = 4	2 × 5 = 10
3 × 2 = 6	3 × 5 = 15
4 × 2 = 8	4 × 5 = 20
5 × 2 = 10	5 × 5 = 25
6 × 2 = 12	6 × 5 = 30
7 × 2 = 14	7 × 5 = 35
8 × 2 = 16	8 × 5 = 40
9 × 2 = 18	9 × 5 = 45
10 × 2 = 20	10 × 5 = 50
11 × 2 = 22	11 × 5 = 55
12 × 2 = 24	12 × 5 = 60

Here are some facts that will help you with multiplication and division by 2, 5 and 10.

All multiples of 2 have a 0, 2, 4, 6 or 8 as their last digit.

All multiples of 5 have a 5 or 0 ones as their last digit.

These facts make it easy to spot multiples of numbers.

- 25 ends in 5, so it's a multiple of 5.
- 18 ends in 8, so it's a multiple of 2.
- 56 ends in 6, so it's a multiple of 2.
- 70 ends in 0 so it is a multiple of 2 and 5.

Tips 💡

If you don't know the answer, draw a number line to help you.

💬 Talk maths

All these numbers are multiples. They belong to the 2- or 5-times table.
Say the multiplication fact for each of these numbers.
Remember to look at the ones digit to help you.

18   ? × ? =   22   ? × ? =   45   ? × ? =

25   ? × ? =   6   ? × ? =

Some multiples belong to more than one multiplication table.

10 is 1 × 10 and 2 × 5 and 5 × 2.

20 is 2 × 10 and 4 × 5 and 10 × 2.

Think of some more multiples that are in the 5- and 10-times table.

✔ Check

1. Write a multiplication fact from the 2- or 5-times table.

   a. 35 ☐ × ☐ = 35   b. 50 ☐ × ☐ = 50

   c. 16 ☐ × ☐ = 16   d. 24 ☐ × ☐ = 24

2. Write a division fact from the 2- or 5-times table.

   a. 6   6 ÷ ☐ = ☐   b. 25   25 ÷ ☐ = ☐

⚠ Problems

Brain-teaser Ava has five boxes of raisins. Each box holds eight raisins.

How many raisins does Ava have in total? ☐

Brain-buster Sophie has 69 marbles. She keeps 39 marbles for herself. She shares out the rest of the marbles between her five sisters.

How many marbles does each sister get? ☐

Multiplication and division

34   35

Unit structure

- **Recap** – a recap of basic facts of the mathematical area in focus.
- **Revise** – examples and facts specific to the age group.
- **Tips** – short and simple advice to aid understanding.
- **Talk maths** – focused activities that encourage verbal practice.
- **Check** – a focused range of questions, with answers at the end of the book.
- **Problems** – word problems requiring mathematics to be used in context.

* Note that Tips and Talk sections are not present in single-page units.

Keep some blank or squared paper handy for notes and calculations!

Using this book at home

Improving your child's maths

It sounds obvious, but this is the best reason for using this book. Whether working sequentially through units, dipping in to resolve confusion, or reinforcing classroom learning, you can use this book to help your child see the benefits and pleasures of being competent in maths.

Consolidating school work

Most schools communicate clearly what they are doing each week via newsletters or homework. Using this book, alongside the maths being done at school, can boost children's mastery of the concepts.

Be sure not to get ahead of schoolwork or to confuse your child. If in doubt, talk to your child's class teacher.

Revising for tests

Regular testing is a fact of life for children these days, like it or not. Improving children's confidence is a good way to avoid stress as well as improve performance. Where children have obvious difficulties, dipping in to the book and focusing on specific facts and skills can be very helpful.

To provide specific practice for end-of-year tests we recommend *National Curriculum Maths Tests* for Year 2.

Do a little, often

Keep sessions to an absolute maximum of 30 minutes. Even if children want to keep going, short amounts of focused study on a regular basis will help to sustain learning and enthusiasm in the long run.

Track progress

The revision tracker chart on page 7 provides a simple way for children to record their progress with this book. Remember, you've really 'got it' when you can understand and apply the maths confidently in different contexts. This means all the questions in the *Check* and *Problems* sections should not present any difficulties.

Avoid confusion

If your child really doesn't seem to understand a particular unit, take a step back. There may be some prior knowledge that s/he does not understand, or it may contradict how they have learned similar facts at school. Try looking at much simpler examples than those given in the book, and if in doubt talk to your child's teacher.

Talk, talk, talk

There is big value in discussing maths, both using vocabulary and explaining concepts. The more children can be encouraged to do this, especially explaining their thinking and understanding, the better the learning. Even if adults understand the work better than children, having them 'teach' you is a great way to consolidate their learning.

Practice makes perfect

Even the world's best footballers have to regularly practise kicking a ball. Brief warm ups before starting a unit, such as rapid recall of times tables or addition facts, or answering a few questions on mathematical vocabulary (see glossary) can help keep children on their toes.

Maths is everywhere – use it!

Children have lots of English lessons at school, and they use language almost constantly in daily life. They also have lots of maths lessons but encounter its use in daily life much less. Involving children in everyday maths is very useful. Shopping and money are the obvious ones, but cooking, decorating, planning holidays, catching buses, to name a few examples, can all involve important mathematical thinking and talk.

Revision tracker

	Not sure	Getting there	Got it!
Count in steps of 2, 5 and 10			
Read and write numbers to 100			
Compare 2-digit numbers and order them correctly			
Say what each digit in a 2-digit number means			
Show numbers on a number line and a hundred square			
Count up or back in tens to solve an addition or subtraction sentence, like 50 − 20 or 50 + 20			
Recall addition and subtraction facts to 20 and use these to derive related facts to 100			
Add and subtract mentally a 2-digit number and ones, a 2-digit number and tens, and two 2-digit numbers			
Use objects, number lines and hundred squares to add and subtract a 2-digit number and ones, a 2-digit number and tens and two 2-digit numbers			
Add three 1-digit numbers			
Use an addition sentence to check a subtraction, and a subtraction sentence to check an addition; solve missing number problems			
Find the answer to addition and subtraction problems			
Recall multiplication and division facts for the 10-times table			
Recall multiplication and division facts for the 2- and 5-times tables			
Identify odd and even numbers			
Use arrays, number lines and multiplication and division facts to solve problems			
Work out addition in any order; but know that I can't work out subtraction in any order			
Work out multiplication in any order; but know that I can't work out division in any order			
Find the fractions $\frac{1}{3}$, $\frac{1}{4}$, $\frac{2}{4}$ and $\frac{3}{4}$ of shapes, numbers and measures			
Use my multiplication tables to help me to find fractions of numbers and quantities			
Find $\frac{2}{4}$ of a shape, measure or number, and know that this is the same as $\frac{1}{2}$			
Compare and order measurements of length, mass and capacity			
Choose and use standard units of length, mass and capacity			
Recognise all the coins to £1 and I know how to record using £ and p; combine coins to make a total			
Tell the time to the nearest 5 minutes			
Put events in order and use the vocabulary of time relating to events such as before, after, next…			
Solve money problems and show my working of how I did this			
Compare and sort 2D shapes			
Compare and sort 3D shapes			
Recognise and name 2D shapes on the faces of 3D shapes			
Make a sequence and a repeating pattern using 2D shapes			
Recognise a right-angle turn; recognise two, three and four right-angle turns			
Make and understand data charts			
Ask and answer questions from data charts			
Make totals and comparisons from data charts			

Counting in steps

↺ Recap

We can count in steps on a number line. Follow these counts with your finger.

Count in 2s.

Count in 5s.

Count in 10s.

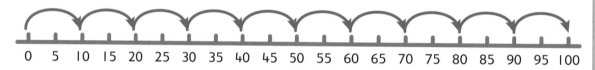

Revise

When you count in steps, all the steps must be the same. Continue to count in 3s on this number line.

Look at this number line.

Now mark counting in 2s from 0 using arrows.

Which numbers are visited by both 2s and 5s?

Why do you think that is?

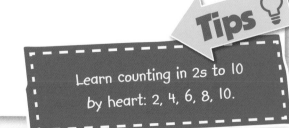

Tips

Learn counting in 2s to 10 by heart: 2, 4, 6, 8, 10.

Talk maths

Say these counts aloud.

What do you notice about the last count?

0	2	4	6	8	10	12	14	16	18	20
0	3	6	9	12	15	18	21	24	27	30
0	5	10	15	20	25	30	35	40	45	50
0	10	20	30	40	50	60	70	80	90	100
6	16	26	36	46	56	66	76	86	96	106

✔ Check

1. **These counts go backwards. Write the missing numbers.**

   a.   20   18   16   ☐   ☐   ☐   8

   b.   18   15   ☐   ☐   ☐   3   0

2. **Write the missing numbers.**

   a.   20   30   40   ☐   ☐   ☐

   b.   35   30   25   ☐   ☐   ☐

3. **Start at 4. Count forward in steps of 10. Write down all the numbers below 100. The first two numbers have been done for you.**

   4, 14, _____

⚠ Problems

Brain-teaser There are nine pairs of shoes in the cupboard.

How many shoes are there altogether?   ☐

Brain-buster Tom puts 10p in his money box every week.

How many weeks will it take for him to save £1?   ☐

Reading and writing numbers to at least 100

↺ Recap

Read the number carefully, beginning with the tens word or digit.

These are all 2-digit numbers.

| 10 | 24 | 31 | 76 | 89 |

Read them aloud.

📋 Revise

Here are the ones words.

one	two	three	four	five	six	seven	eight	nine
1	2	3	4	5	6	7	8	9

These number words come next.

ten	eleven	twelve	thirteen	fourteen	fifteen
10	11	12	13	14	15

sixteen	seventeen	eighteen	nineteen
16	17	18	19

Here are the tens words.

ten	twenty	thirty	forty	fifty	sixty	seventy	eighty	ninety
10	20	30	40	50	60	70	80	90

Now we can put the ones words and the tens words together to make other numbers.

21	34	63	95
twenty-one	thirty-four	sixty-three	ninety-five

Tips 💡

When writing a 2-digit number in words, remember the hyphen: twenty-nine

💬 Talk maths

Read these numbers aloud.

| thirty-one | fifty-six | ninety-seven | eighty-one | seventy |

Now say these.

47   81   72   19   44

✔ Check

1. Read the number words. Write the number.

a. fifty-three ☐

b. ninety-nine ☐

c. six ☐

d. thirty-four ☐

e. twenty-two ☐

f. one hundred ☐

2. Now write these numbers in words.

a. 81 _____

b. 14 _____

c. 62 _____

d. 38 _____

e. 90 _____

f. 47 _____

⚠ Problems

Brain-teaser John does his homework. He writes some numbers in words. Mark the spelling for him with a ✔ or ✗

a. fourty-six   **b.** ninety-eight   **c.** twenty-one   **d.** fivety-six

Brain-buster Lucy writes an even number between 56 and 60 in words. What could it be?

_____

11

Comparing and ordering numbers

↺ Recap

Look at the number 18.

We can say the number that is one more than 18. It is 19.

We can say the number that is one less than 18. It is 17.

📄 Revise

When comparing numbers, look at the tens digit first.

3 tens is greater than 2 tens.

36 is greater than **2**9.

If both tens digits are the same, look at the ones digit.

2**3** is greater than 2**1**.

tens	ones	tens	ones
3	6	2	9

< means **is less than**	> means **is greater than**	= means **is equal to**

These number sentences are true.

48 > 39

82 < 94

11 – 5 < 15

7 + 8 = 18 – 3

We can order 2-digit numbers from smallest to largest or from largest to smallest.

From smallest number to largest:

13   15   27   93

smallest   largest

💡 Tips

Remember, always look at the tens digits first. This will help you to decide which number is larger. If both numbers have the same tens digit, look at the ones digit. Now you can decide which is the larger number.

From largest number to smallest:

93   27   15   13

largest   smallest

💬 Talk maths

Look at these number sentences and read them aloud.

36 > 29   29 < 43

They read: 36 is larger than 29, and 29 is smaller than 43. We can order these numbers from smallest to largest or the other way round.

Here are the numbers ordered smallest to largest: 29, 36, 43.

Here are the numbers ordered the other way around, largest to smallest: 43, 36, 29.

Say the numbers aloud in each order.

Complete the Check section below, then read each number sentence aloud.

✔ Check

1. **Write <, >, = or a number to make these number sentences true.**

    a. 64 ☐ 73

    b. 13 + 7 ☐ 20

    c. 45 ☐ 44

    d. 33 − 7 = ☐ + 21

2. **Write these numbers in order, starting with the smallest number.**

64   91   37   72   59 _____

⚠ Problems

Brain-teaser Delun has 34 sweets, Bella has 43 sweets and Jamie has 24 sweets.

Who has the fewest sweets? _____

Brain-buster Jon has fewer than 50 sweets but more than each of the three children in the Brain-teaser.

How many sweets could Jon have? ☐

Recognising place value in 2-digit numbers

↻ Recap

2-digit numbers are made from a tens digit and a ones digit.

📋 Revise

A 2-digit number can also be made on an abacus.

tens ones

Count the tens to give you the tens number. Ten, twenty, thirty.

Now count the ones on the abacus to give you the ones number.

One, two, three, four, five.

The abacus shows 35.

Here is another abacus. Read the number.

tens ones

5 tens and 4 ones... it's 54!

Now show 37 on this abacus.

tens ones

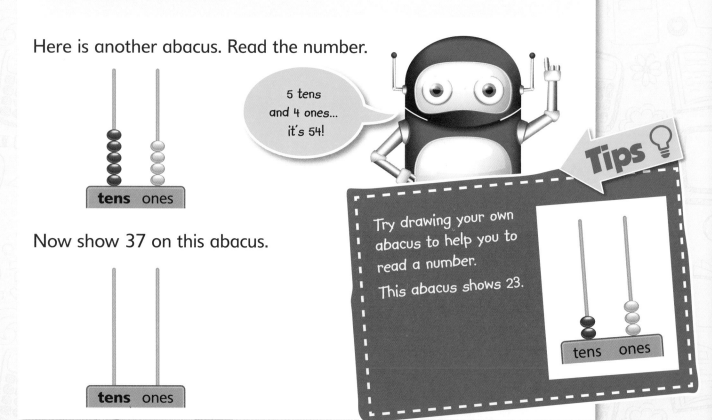

Tips

Try drawing your own abacus to help you to read a number.

This abacus shows 23.

tens ones

 **Talk maths**

Here are some numbers made with tens and ones.

Say each number aloud.   30 and 5   40 and 6   70 and 8

We can write these using just one digit for the tens and one digit
for the ones.   35   46   78

Try saying some other numbers aloud and challenge a partner
to write them.

✔ Check

1. **Write the 2-digit numbers for this abacus.** _____

2. **Show 51 on this abacus.**

3. **Circle the largest tens digit. Put a cross under the smallest one digit.**

    45   26   61   53

⚠ Problems

Darina

Mina

Brain-teaser How many more is on Darina's abacus than on Mina's?

Brain-buster Tamsin shows 74 on an abacus. She adds one more ring to the
tens. Then she adds three more rings to the ones.

What number does the abacus show now?

Showing numbers in different ways

↺ Recap

Numbers can be shown in different ways.

Here are all the numbers from 1 to 100 on a hundred square.

1	2	3	4	5	6	7	8	9	10
11	12	13	14	15	16	17	18	19	20
21	22	23	24	25	26	27	28	29	30
31	32	33	34	35	36	37	38	39	40
41	42	43	44	45	46	47	48	49	50
51	52	53	54	55	56	57	58	59	60
61	62	63	64	65	66	67	68	69	70
71	72	73	74	75	76	77	78	79	80
81	82	83	84	85	86	87	88	89	90
91	92	93	94	95	96	97	98	99	100

What is the number that is one before 100?

It's 99!

🗒 Revise

Look at the hundred square above.

Count along the top row.

These are the numbers from 1 to 10.

Now count down the last column in tens.

These are the tens numbers from 10 to 100.

Count along the top row from 1 to 5, then count down the 5 column:
5, 15, 25, 35, 45, 55, 65, 75, 85, 95.

You can also use a number line to show where a number is.

The arrow points to where 55 belongs.

 *Talk maths*

Look at this number line.

```
20                    ↑            ↑            30
```

The first arrow is halfway along the line.
This means that the number is 25.

What number is the second arrow pointing to?
This number is greater than 25 and less than 30.
It is nearer to 30 than to 25.

> Discuss with a friend or an adult how you know the answer.

✔ Check

1. **Look carefully at the number line. Write in where you estimate the number 43 is.**

```
40                                        50
```

2. **Look at the hundred square.**

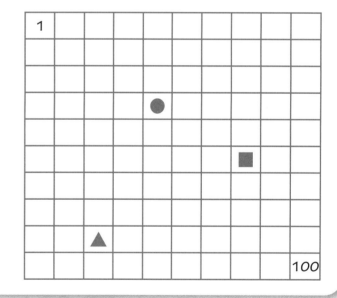

a. Which number is represented by the ●? ☐

b. Which number is represented by the ■? ☐

c. Which number is represented by the ▲? ☐

⚠ Problems

Brain-teaser Peter draws a number line. He marks in 40 and 50. He asks Jake to estimate where 42 is. Write in your estimate of where 42 is.

```
40                                        50
```

Using place value and number facts to solve problems

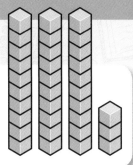

↻ Recap

These cubes show three groups of ten and three ones.
That is 33.

📋 Revise

Think about the number facts that you know using ones.

Look at this number sentence.   6 + 3 = 9

We can use this number fact to solve 60 + 30.

If 6 + 3 = 9, then 60 + 30 = 90.

Let's try a subtraction. What about   40 − ☐ = 10

We know that 4 − 3 = 1.

Can you use this to work out the missing number?

Another way to solve this is to use a number line.

💡 Tips

So if the question is 60 − ☐ = 20, try 6 − 4 = 2 to help you.

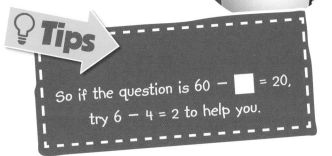

You can also solve this by counting up from 10 to 40, in tens.

Check how many tens you count. Counting up from 10, we would count 20, 30, 40. That's three tens, so the answer is 30.

Now addition. Look at this calculation.   30 + ☐ = 50

You can use a number line to solve this by counting up from 30 to 50.
So 30 + 20 = 50

And of course, we could have used 3 + 2 = 5 to work out this answer.

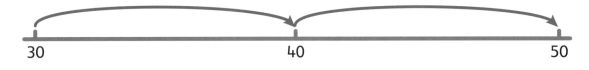

💬 Talk maths

Count along these number lines, saying the missing numbers to answer the questions.

20 + ? = 60

20   60

80 − ? = 40

40   80

70 − 10 = ?

10   70

✔ Check

1. **Use place value and number facts to solve these calculations.**

   a. 50 − ⬜ = 40   **b.** 20 + ⬜ = 70   **c.** 90 − ⬜ = 10

   d. 70 − ⬜ = 30   **e.** 30 + ⬜ = 100   **f.** 40 + ⬜ = 90

⚠ Problems

Brain-teaser Tom has 40 marbles. Jake has 70 marbles.

How many more marbles has Jake than Tom? ⬜

Brain-buster Sally has 30 beads and Jane has 40 beads.

They want to make a necklace of 90 beads.

How many more beads do they need? ⬜

Addition and subtraction facts to 20 and related facts to 100

↺ Recap

Here are some number facts that you already know.

> 2 + 6 = 8
> 7 + 3 = 10
> 14 − 9 = 5
> 16 + 2 = 18

You can use these number facts to help you to find other addition and subtraction facts.

📋 Revise

You can use facts you know to find other facts like this.

| 7 + 9 = 16 | so | 16 − 7 = 9 | or | 16 − 9 = 7 |

| 9 + 7 = 16 | so | 16 − 9 = 7 | or | 16 − 7 = 9 |

So you know that 7 + 9 = 16 .

You can use that fact to work out that 27 + 9 = 36 .

Then you can work out other facts like this, using these numbers.

> 9 + 27 = 36
> 36 − 9 = 27
> 36 − 27 = 9

Here's another fact you know.

15 − 6 = 9

So 25 − 6 = 19.

And 25 − 16 = 9.

Let's do one more.

14 + 5 = 19

So 34 + 5 = 39.

And 34 + 15 = 49.

Draw a number line and count on to check your answers.

Tips 💡

Remember to use the number facts that you do know to find the answer.

🗩 Talk maths

You know that 9 + 6 = 15.
So 19 + 6 = 25.
And 29 + 6 = 35.

Here are some more.
39 + 6 = 45
49 + 6 = 55
Discuss the pattern with
a friend.

Let's try a subtraction.
6 − 4 = 2
So 16 − 4 = 12.
26 − 14 = 12   36 − 24 = 12

All these facts use your
knowledge that 6 − 4 = 2.

✔ Check

1. **Complete these calculations.**

a. 12 + 6 = ☐

So 22 + 6 = ☐

b. 14 − 12 = ☐

So 24 − 2 = ☐

c. 9 + 6 = ☐

So 29 + 6 = ☐

d. 18 − 9 = ☐

So 38 − 9 = ☐

e. 12 + 7 = ☐

So 32 + 7 = ☐

⚠ Problems

Brain-teaser Mike has 12 marbles and Tom has 4. They have 16 marbles altogether.

John has 22 marbles and Phil has 4.

How many marbles do they have altogether? ☐

Brain-buster Jade has 14 pens. She gives Sam three pens. Now Jade has 11 pens left.

Sally has 44 pens. She gives Lin 23 pens.

How many pens does Sally have now? ☐

Adding and subtracting mentally

↻ Recap

You know lots of number facts already.

| 15 + 4 = 19 | 17 − 15 = 2 | 12 + 6 = 18 | 20 − 7 = 13 |

You can use these number facts to help you to find other facts.

📋 Revise

Here are some ideas for adding or subtracting mentally.

64 + 5 . You can use 4 + 5 = 9 to solve this.

So 64 + 5 = 69.

Let's look at 59 − 7 .
Well, you know that 9 − 7 = 2.
So 59 − 7 = 52.

When adding a 2-digit number and tens, count on in tens.

43 add 30 is 53, 63, 73. 43 + 30 = 73.

Or add the 4 tens and the 3 tens in your head to make 70 then add back the 3 ones to make 73.

For subtracting tens from a 2-digit number:
36 − 10 is 26.
So 36 − 20 is 16.
And 36 − 30 is 6.

To add two 2-digit numbers add the tens first then the ones. So for 51 + 33, add 50 and 30 to make 80, then 1 and 3 to make 4. That equals 84.

Let's try a subtraction: 56 subtract 34 .
Subtract the tens first, then the ones.
We use 5 − 3 = 2 to help with subtracting the tens.
50 − 30 = 20
And 6 − 4 = 2 can be used for subtracting the ones.
So 56 − 34 = 22.

Tips

Remember when working mentally you can count on or back in ones or tens, or add or subtract the tens, and then the ones.

💬 *Talk maths*

Talk through these examples with an adult.

24 + 5   We know that 4 + 5 = 9, so 24 + 5 = 29.

35 − 4   5 − 4 = 1, so 35 − 4 = 31.

54 + 20   It is just the tens that will change here, not the ones.
               We know that 5 + 2 = 7, so 50 + 20 = 70 and 54 + 20 = 74.

54 − 20   Just the tens will change here.
               5 − 2 = 3, so 50 − 20 = 30 and so 54 − 20 = 34.

34 + 21   3 + 2 = 5, so 30 + 20 = 50.
               4 + 1 = 5
               Let's put those together. 34 + 21 = 55.

67 − 25   6 − 2 = 4, so 60 − 20 = 40.
               7 − 5 = 2
               Put those together. 67 − 25 = 42.

✔ Check

1. **Work the answers out mentally.**

a. 46 + 3 = ☐   b. 55 + 40 = ☐   c. 67 − 26 = ☐

d. 98 − 7 = ☐   e. 36 + 23 = ☐   f. 84 − 22 = ☐

⚠ Problems

Brain-teaser There are 24 swap cards in the pile.
James puts another 20 swap cards on the pile.

How many swap cards are there altogether? ☐

Brain-buster Marta has 55 swap cards. She gives her sister 23 of her cards.

How many cards does Marta have left? ☐

Adding and subtracting by using objects and representations

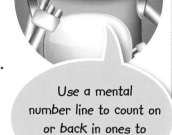

↺ Recap

9 + 7 Make a 10, and then count on the rest.
9 and 1 is 10. Another 6 makes 16. So 9 + 7 = 16.

18 − 9 Take away 8 from 18 to leave 10.
1 more to take away, so the answer is 9.

> Use a mental number line to count on or back in ones to help you.

📝 Revise

Adding 2-digit numbers and ones

54 + 7 54 and 6 is 60 and 1 more is 61. So 54 + 7 = 61.
You could also use a hundred square. Find 54 on a hundred square.
Now count to the next 10 (60). You have added 6.
Now count on 1 more so that 7 is added. The answer is 61.

Subtracting 2-digit numbers and ones

54 − 7 Subtract 4 to reach 50. Then subtract the remaining 3.
The answer is 47.

−3   −4

45   46   47   48   49   50   51   52   53   54   55

Adding a 2-digit number and tens

43 + 30 Add the tens digit first. Use a hundred square to count on.
40 + 30 is 40 and 50, 60, 70. So 40 + 30 = 70. Add on the 3: 43 + 30 = 73

Adding two 2-digit numbers

36 + 28 Start by adding the tens. 36 + 28 ➜ 36 + 20 + 8 ➜ 56 + 8 = 64

+20   +8

35 36 37 38 39 40 41 42 43 44 45 46 47 48 49 50 51 52 53 54 55 56 57 58 59 60 61 62 63 64 65

Finding the difference between two 2-digit numbers

64 − 39 Count up from 39 on a number line like this. So 64 − 39 = 25

+1   +20   +4

35 36 37 38 39 40 41 42 43 44 45 46 47 48 49 50 51 52 53 54 55 56 57 58 59 60 61 62 63 64 65

💬 *Talk maths*

Look at each number sentence.

Talk about how you would find the answer.

62 + 8	35 + 40	32 + 43
51 − 4	67 − 50	72 − 55

Tips

Choose the best method for you. This may not be the same as your friends.

✔ Check

1. **Choose how you will find the answer.**
   Write this out each time.

   a. 63 + 8 = ☐

   b. 97 − 8 = ☐

   c. 45 + 20 = ☐

   d. 65 − 30 = ☐

   e. 47 + 21 = ☐

   f. 64 − 36 = ☐

⚠ Problems

Brain-teaser Tim has 63 marbles.

He lends 45 marbles to Sam.

How many marbles does Tim have now? ☐

Brain-buster Paula gave Marcus 25 sweets.

She has 26 sweets left.

How many sweets did Paula have
before she gave some to Marcus? ☐

Adding three 1-digit numbers

↺ Recap

Here are 3 cubes and 6 cubes.
We can use them to work out 3 + 6.
Put the 3 cubes and the 6 cubes
together to make 9.
So 3 + 6 = 9.

📄 Revise

Here are some ideas for adding three 1-digit numbers.

Make a 10

6 + 4 + 8   6 + 4 is 10   10 + 8 is 18
We can also use this for 3 + 6 + 7.
Put the numbers into a different order to help make 10.
3 + 7 + 6 = 10 + 6 = 16.

Look for doubles

7 + 7 + 4   7 + 7 is 14   14 + 4 is 18
9 + 5 + 9   9 + 9 is 18.
18 + 5 can be seen as 18 + 2 + 3.
18 + 2 = 20.
20 + 3 = 23

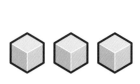
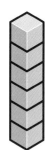

Draw a number line to help you.
For a subtraction that has a missing number, count on from the lower to the higher number to give the missing number.
This works for addition too!

Choose the best order to add

When adding three 1-digit numbers, decide which is the best order for you to add them.

6 + 5 + 6   6 + 6 is 12   12 + 5 = 17

Use objects and diagrams

You can also use cubes, number lines and hundred squares to help you add three 1-digit numbers.

💬 Talk maths

Say how you would do each of these.
Remember, you are working mentally.
Now work out the answer for each one.
Explain how you worked.

Tips 💡

Remember when working mentally you can add three 1-digit numbers in any order.

| 5 + 5 + 6 | 3 + 9 + 3 | 4 + 8 + 7 | 9 + 2 + 6 |

✔ Check

1. Work the answers out mentally.

a. 2 + 2 + 4 = ☐

b. 7 + 2 + 3 = ☐

2. Choose how you will find the answer to these.

Write your methods.

a. 7 + 6 + 7 = ☐

b. 2 + 9 + 8 = ☐

c. 5 + 2 + 9 = ☐

⚠ Problems

Brain-teaser Tom has 4 football cards.

Dilshad has 6 football cards.

Mark has 8 football cards.

How many cards do they have in total? ☐

Brain-buster Mark puts down 7 marbles.

Sam puts down 5 marbles.

Peter puts down 8 marbles.

How many marbles is that in total? ☐

Checking calculations and missing number problems

13 + 6 = 19 and 6 + 13 = 19
19 − 13 = 6 and 19 − 6 = 13

> If you work out a calculation, then you can find others.

Revise

12 + 7 = 19   Check with 19 − 12 = 7.
7 + 12 = 19   Check with 19 − 7 = 12.

This always works for addition and subtraction.

Let's try a different calculation.

23 + 5 = 28   Check with 28 − 5 = 23.
5 + 23 = 28   Check with 28 − 23 = 5.

> You can check your answers for addition by working out a subtraction using the same numbers.

If you start with subtraction, then you can find addition sentences in the same way.

28 − 7 = 21   Check with 7 + 21 = 28.
28 − 21 = 7   Check with 21 + 7 = 28.

If you are not sure break the numbers down like this.

35 + 12 = 47   35 + 12 = 30 + 5 + 10 + 2 = 40 + 7 = 47
Then 12 + 35 = 47   47 − 35 = 12   47 − 12 = 35

Let's try a subtraction this time.   58 − 16 = 42
Or 58 − 16 = 50 − 10 + 8 − 6 = 42

Some questions have missing numbers. Here's a calculation to try.

25 + [ ] = 32

You can count up in your head or draw a number line like this.

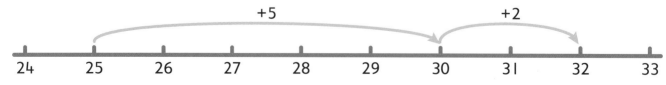

So counting on the number line gives 5 + 2 = 7. So 25 + 7 = 32.

 **Talk maths**

We can use what we know about the link between addition and subtraction to check answers. Work out the answers to these questions. Discuss with a friend or adult how you know the answer.

| 42 + 7 = 49 | 49 − 7 = ? |
| 51 − 8 = 43 | 43 + 8 = ? |

Tips

Draw a number line to help you. For a subtraction that has a missing number, count on from the lower to the higher number to give the missing number. This works for addition too!

✔ Check

Sara has done some homework.

She is not sure that her answers are correct.

Write a check calculation for the homework calculations.

Then put a tick or a cross for Sara's answers.

	Sara's answers	Check calculations	✔ or ✗
1	12 + 7 = 19		
2	21 + 9 = 29		
3	35 − 4 = 31		
4	24 + 13 = 27		
5	54 − 23 = 31		

⚠ Problems

Brain-teaser Elsie has 64 beads. She counts the blue beads. There are 32 blue beads. She thinks that 32 beads are red.

Write a calculation to show whether Elsie is correct. _____

Write a check calculation too. _____

Brain-buster There are 35 biscuits in the tin. Eva adds another 24 biscuits. Then Eva eats 4 biscuits. Eva thinks there are now 55 biscuits in the tin.

Write a check calculation to show whether Eva is correct. _____

_____

Solving problems with addition and subtraction

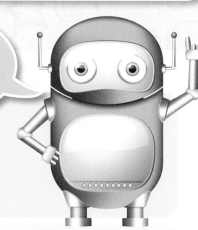

↻ Recap

Here are some words that you may find in problems, with their meanings.

Means add

put together	altogether	total	how many

Means subtract

how many more	how many fewer	less than

how much change	difference between	distance between

Revise

Read the problem carefully. Look for the key words in the problem.

Mary has five brothers and four sisters.

How many children are there in Mary's family?

Don't forget to add in Mary!

So 5 brothers + 4 sisters + 1 Mary = 5 + 4 + 1 = 10

Read this problem carefully. Think about how you would solve it.

A box of cherries costs 65p. How much change will I get from £1?

To solve this, subtract 65p from £1.

Don't forget to change the £1 to 100 pennies.

You could use a number line like this.

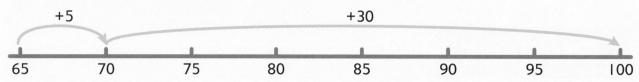

+5   +30

65   70   75   80   85   90   95   100

Counting up from 65 to 100 gives us 5 + 30, or 35.

So the change is 35p.

Tips

Underline the key words and numbers in the problem. Then you have all the key facts.

💬 *Talk maths*

Read aloud the problems in the boxes.
The key words and numbers are highlighted.

John is reading some comics.
One comic has 45 pages and the other one has 39 pages.
How many pages is that altogether?

How many and altogether tell us this is an add problem. So 45 + 39.

Sarah has 14 goldfish in a fish tank.
She also has 26 goldfish in the garden pond.
How many more goldfish does Sarah need to make 50?

To solve this problem we need to find out how many goldfish Sarah has now.

So 14 + 26 = 10 + 20 + 4 + 6 = 30 + 10 = 40. Sarah has 40 goldfish.

The problem asks how many more goldfish Sarah needs to make 50.

So 50 − 40 = 10. ➡ Sarah needs 10 more goldfish.

✔ Check

Problem	Working	Answer
1. There are 27 kittens and 19 puppies at the rescue centre. How many are there in total?		
2. 64 children wanted to go to the cinema. There were just 35 tickets left. How many children did not get a ticket?		

⚠ Problems

Brain-teaser Lollies cost 10p each and ice creams cost 25p each.
Josh buys one lolly and two ice creams. How much does he spend? ☐ p

31

Multiplication and division facts for the 10-times table

↻ Recap

Let's count in tens.

0   10   20   30   40   50   60   70   80   90   100   110   120

These numbers are used in the 10-times table.

📋 Revise

These are the signs that are used in multiplication and division.

× means multiply.   ÷ means divide.

Remember the word **multiple**. It means the answer when you multiply. So, in the 10-times table the multiples are 0, 10, 20, 30, 40, 50, 60, 70, 80, 90, 100, 110, 120.

10-times table	Dividing by 10
$1 \times 10 = 10$	$10 \div 10 = 1$
$2 \times 10 = 20$	$20 \div 10 = 2$
$3 \times 10 = 30$	$30 \div 10 = 3$
$4 \times 10 = 40$	$40 \div 10 = 4$
$5 \times 10 = 50$	$50 \div 10 = 5$
$6 \times 10 = 60$	$60 \div 10 = 6$
$7 \times 10 = 70$	$70 \div 10 = 7$
$8 \times 10 = 80$	$80 \div 10 = 8$
$9 \times 10 = 90$	$90 \div 10 = 9$
$10 \times 10 = 100$	$100 \div 10 = 10$
$11 \times 10 = 110$	$110 \div 10 = 11$
$12 \times 10 = 120$	$120 \div 10 = 12$

All multiples in the 10-times table have a 0 ones digit.

Which of these numbers are in the 10-times table?

15   90   25   40

Look at the ones digit. Only if it is a 0 will it be in the 10-times table. So the answer is 90 and 40.

Tips 💡

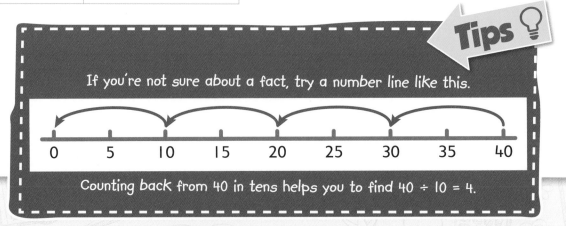

If you're not sure about a fact, try a number line like this.

0   5   10   15   20   25   30   35   40

Counting back from 40 in tens helps you to find $40 \div 10 = 4$.

💬 Talk maths

Look carefully at this set of four number sentences.
Say each number sentence.

| 10 × 5 = 50 | 5 × 10 = 50 | 50 ÷ 10 = 5 | 50 ÷ 5 = 10 |

All these number sentences are made from the multiplication fact
10 × 5 = 50.

Now say the first number sentence below.
Use the numbers to complete the others in the set.

9 × 10 = 90   10 × ? = 90

90 ÷ ? = 9   90 ÷ ? = 10

Remember, if you know a multiplication sentence you can use those
numbers to make another multiplication and two division sentences.

✔ Check

1. **Complete these
    times tables facts.**

a. 6 × 10 = ☐

b. 3 × 10 = ☐

c. 10 × 10 = ☐

d. 50 ÷ 10 = ☐

e. 90 ÷ 10 = ☐

⚠ Problems

Brain-teaser Jane has four packs of
10 pens.

How many pens is that in total?

Brain-buster Mya buys six packs of pens.
Each pack has 10 pens. Mya gives two packs
of pens to her sister.

How many pens does Mya have now?

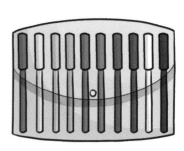

Multiplication and division facts for the 2- and 5-times tables

Here is the count in 2s.

0   2   4   6   8   10   12   14   16   18   20   22   24

This count in 2s is used in the 2-times table.

And here is the count in 5s.

0   5   10   15   20   25   30   35   40   45   50   55   60

This count in 5s is used in the 5-times table.

📝 Revise

2-times table	5-times table
1 × 2 = 2	1 × 5 = 5
2 × 2 = 4	2 × 5 = 10
3 × 2 = 6	3 × 5 = 15
4 × 2 = 8	4 × 5 = 20
5 × 2 = 10	5 × 5 = 25
6 × 2 = 12	6 × 5 = 30
7 × 2 = 14	7 × 5 = 35
8 × 2 = 16	8 × 5 = 40
9 × 2 = 18	9 × 5 = 45
10 × 2 = 20	10 × 5 = 50
11 × 2 = 22	11 × 5 = 55
12 × 2 = 24	12 × 5 = 60

Here are some facts that will help you with multiplication and division by 2, 5 and 10.

All multiples of 2 have a 0, 2, 4, 6 or 8 as their last digit.

All multiples of 5 have a 5 or 0 ones as their last digit.

These facts make it easy to spot multiples of numbers.

- 25 ends in 5, so it's a multiple of 5.
- 18 ends in 8, so it's a multiple of 2.
- 56 ends in 6, so it's a multiple of 2.
- 70 ends in 0 so it is a multiple of 2 and 5.

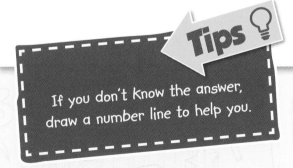

Tips 💡

If you don't know the answer, draw a number line to help you.

💬 Talk maths

All these numbers are multiples. They belong to the 2- or 5-times table.

Say the multiplication fact for each of these numbers.

Remember to look at the ones digit to help you.

18   ? × ? =   22   ? × ? =   45   ? × ? =

25   ? × ? =   6   ? × ? =

Some multiples belong to more than one multiplication table.

10 is 1 × 10 and 2 × 5 and 5 × 2.

20 is 2 × 10 and 4 × 5 and 10 × 2.

Think of some more multiples that are in the 5- and 10-times table.

✔ Check

1. **Write a multiplication fact from the 2- or 5-times table.**

    a. 35 [ ] × [ ] = 35   **b.** 50 [ ] × [ ] = 50

    c. 16 [ ] × [ ] = 16   **d.** 24 [ ] × [ ] = 24

2. **Write a division fact from the 2- or 5-times table.**

    a. 6   6 ÷ [ ] = [ ]   **b.** 25   25 ÷ [ ] = [ ]

⚠ Problems

Brain-teaser Ava has five boxes of raisins. Each box holds eight raisins.

How many raisins does Ava have in total? [ ]

Brain-buster Sophie has 69 marbles. She keeps 39 marbles for herself.
She shares out the rest of the marbles between her five sisters.

How many marbles does each sister get? [ ]

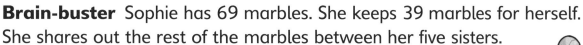

Odd and even numbers

↻ Recap

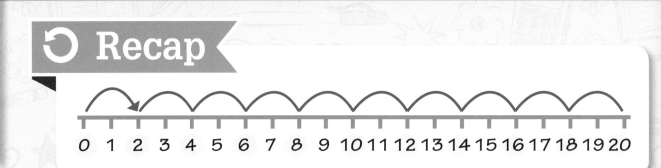

0 1 2 3 4 5 6 7 8 9 10 11 12 13 14 15 16 17 18 19 20

📋 Revise

Numbers can be put into two groups.

Even numbers always have a ones digit of 0, 2, 4, 6, or 8.

Odd numbers always have a ones digit of 1, 3, 5, 7 or 9.

Look at the number line above for counting in 2s.

The numbers landed on are the even numbers.

0, 2, 4, 6, 8, 10, 12, 14, 16, 18, 20

The numbers that are not in the count of 2s are the odd numbers.

1, 3, 5, 7, 9, 11, 13, 15, 17, 19

Look at these two sets of numbers.

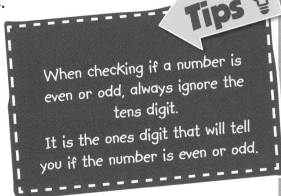

Tips 💡

When checking if a number is even or odd, always ignore the tens digit.

It is the ones digit that will tell you if the number is even or odd.

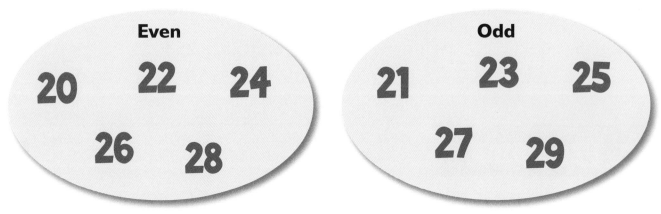

Always check the ones digit of a number to see if it is odd or even.

So, 25 has 5 as its ones digit and is odd.

24 has 4 as its ones digit and is even.

💬 Talk maths

Say the even numbers in this set.   24   31   63   48

Explain how you know.

Which are the odd numbers? How do you know?

Look at this set of cubes.

Count the cubes.

Now count them in 2s.
2, 4, 6 and so on.

You should find that there is one cube left over because 15 is an odd number.

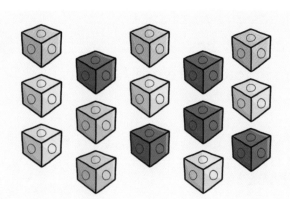

✔ Check

1. **Put a circle round the even numbers.**   92   73   80   47

2. **Put a circle round the odd numbers.**   46   83   24   7

3. **Is 64 odd or even?** _____

4. **Is 89 odd or even?** _____

5. **Add 5 to 7. Is the answer odd or even?** _____

⚠ Problems

Brain-teaser Jamie says he has an odd number of football cards. The number is less than 75 but more than 72.

How many football cards does Jamie have? [   ]

Brain-buster There are 12 pigeons on the ground. Five sparrows are sitting on the fence. Six doves are watching from the rooftop.

Is the total number of birds odd or even? [   ]

Solving problems involving multiplication and division

↺ Recap

Here is an array.

It has 2 rows of spots.
Each row has 5 spots in it.
So in total there are 10 spots.

📝 Revise

$5 × 7 = 35$ $7 × 5 = 35$
$35 ÷ 5 = 7$ $35 ÷ 7 = 5$

You can make arrays to show multiplication and division like this.

Look at this multiplication array.

How many rows of spots are there? How many columns of spots are there?

So 5 rows and 3 columns of spots gives 15 spots in total.
$5 × 3 = 15$
Or $3 × 5 = 15$

💡 Tips

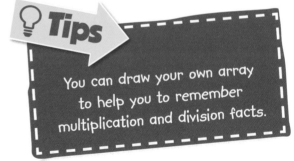

You can draw your own array to help you to remember multiplication and division facts.

Division can be found from arrays too.
Count the number of rows. Count the number of columns.
So $15 ÷ 5 = 3$ and $15 ÷ 3 = 5$.

Draw the array for $6 × 2$.
$12 ÷ 2 = 6$ and $12 ÷ 6 = 2$.

Now you have
$6 × 2 = 12$ and
$2 × 6 = 12$.

🗨 Talk maths

Look at this array.

How many spots are there altogether?
Say the two multiplication facts.
Say the two division facts.
This array gives 3 × 10 = 30 and 10 × 3 = 30.
30 ÷ 3 = 10 and 30 ÷ 10 = 3.

✔ Check

1. **On a separate piece of paper, draw the array for these calculations. Write the total each time.**

   a. 5 × 2 　　　　**b.** 6 × 5 　　　　**c.** 2 × 10

2. **Now draw the array for these.**
   Write two multiplication sentences for each array.
   Write two division sentences for each array.

   a. 7 × 2 　　　　**b.** 4 × 5 　　　　**c.** 3 × 10

⚠ Problems

Brain-teaser Bethany wants to make a patio in her garden. She has 12 paving slabs. She makes an array where one row has 6 slabs.

Write two multiplication facts for the array.

☐ × ☐ = ☐　　　☐ × ☐ = ☐

Brain-buster Max has some counters.

He makes an array with them. There are 6 counters in a row. There are 5 counters in a column.

How many counters are there altogether? ☐

Adding numbers in any order

↺ Recap

Look at these numbers.   5, 6, 11

We can make two addition and two subtraction sentences with these numbers.

5 + 6 = 11   6 + 5 = 11   11 − 5 = 6   11 − 6 = 5

📋 Revise

Here are two sets.

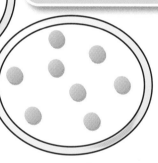

Addition can be done in any order. 26 + 13 = 39
13 + 26 = 39

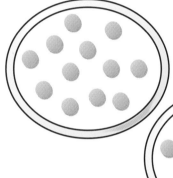

There are 12 in one set and 8 in the other. Now add these. Your total should be 20. So 12 + 8 = 20.

Now do this again, this time starting with the set of 8. 8 + 12 = 20. You have the same answer. So it does not matter which order you add in.

Now look at subtraction.

12 − 8 = 4

Look what happens if you start with 8. This would give a different answer! 8 − 12.

So the order in which you subtract **does** matter.

✔ Check

1. Look at each of these pairs of number sentences.

✔ the ones with the correct answers. Use ✗ for the wrong answers.

a.   15 + 5 = 5 + 15

b.   12 − 4 = 4 − 12

c.   19 + 23 = 23 + 19

d.   36 − 45 = 45 − 36

e.   37 + 46 = 46 + 37

⚠ Problems

Brain-teaser Zikri has £1. He spends 36p. He writes a number sentence to show how much many he has left, 100p − 36p = 64p.

Write an addition number sentence to show that he is correct.

_____

Multiplying numbers in any order

↻ Recap

Look carefully at these multiplication facts.

$2 \times 5 = 10$ $5 \times 2 = 10$

We can multiply numbers in any order:
2×5 gives the same answer as 5×2.

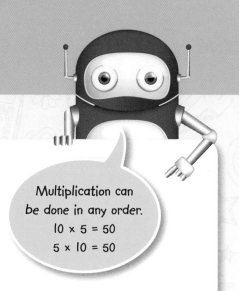

Multiplication can be done in any order.
$10 \times 5 = 50$
$5 \times 10 = 50$

📋 Revise

Here are two multiplications that use the same numbers.
$3 \times 10 = 30$ and $10 \times 3 = 30$.

Now look what happens with division.
$30 \div 10 = 3$
$10 \div 30 = ?$ The answer here cannot be 3.

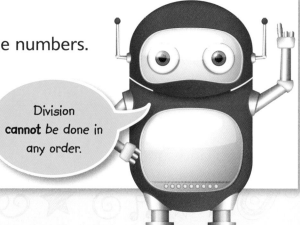

Division **cannot** be done in any order.

✔ Check

1. Write two multiplication sentences for each set of numbers.

a. 5, 2, 10 _____ _____

b. 5, 10, 50 _____ _____

c. 2, 3, 6 _____ _____

d. 5, 8, 40 _____ _____

⚠ Problems

Brain-teaser Jim shares 15 biscuits equally between five plates. Jim writes a number sentence for the sharing. $15 \div 5 = 3$. Write a multiplication number sentence to show that the answer is correct.

☐ × ☐ = ☐

Fractions of shapes

↻ Recap

This square is cut into two equal pieces.
Each of these is worth one half.

$\frac{1}{2}$

This square is divided into four equal pieces.
Each of these is worth one quarter.

$\frac{1}{4}$

Revise

Look at the square cut into quarters.

We write this like this. $\frac{1}{4}$

- So one square is $\frac{1}{4}$ or one out of four.
- Two squares are $\frac{2}{4}$ or two out of four.
- Three squares are $\frac{3}{4}$ or three out of four.
- Four pieces of the square make one whole.

Tips

The bottom number in a fraction tells you how many equal parts the shape has been divided into.
The top number tells you how many of the parts to take.

Look at the circle. It has been cut into quarters.

- So one piece of the circle is a quarter or $\frac{1}{4}$.
- Two pieces of the circle are two quarters or $\frac{2}{4}$.
- Three pieces of the circle are three quarters or $\frac{3}{4}$.
- Four pieces of the circle make a whole one.

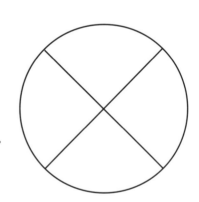

This cake has been cut into three equal slices.
One slice of cake is a third of the cake, or $\frac{1}{3}$.
If you eat all the cake, you have eaten a whole one.

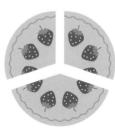

There are four equal pieces in this pizza.
Sophia takes one of the four pieces.
That is a quarter or $\frac{1}{4}$.

💬 Talk maths

Here is a rectangle.

Count how many equal pieces there are altogether.

Now count how many pieces have been shaded.

Say it as a fraction to a friend or adult.

Here is a square.

Count how many equal pieces there are.

Now count how many equal pieces have been shaded.

Can you say the fraction that is unshaded?

✔ Check

1. **Write the fraction that has been shaded for each of these shapes.**

a.
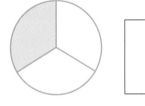

b.
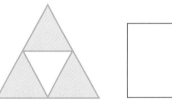

c.

d.
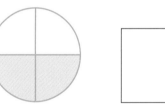

⚠ Problems

Brain-teaser Paul draws a rectangle. He draws lines to make four equal small rectangles inside his rectangle. He shades in two small rectangles.

What fraction has Paul shaded?

Brain-buster Martha bought a pizza for supper for her and Tom. Martha cut the pizza into four equal slices. She ate one slice. Tom ate two slices.

What fraction of the pizza was left?

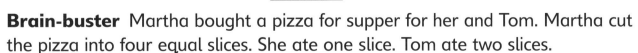

Finding fractions of numbers and quantities

↺ Recap

Remember

$\frac{1}{2}$ means one half or one out of two equal pieces.

$\frac{1}{3}$ means one third or one out of three equal pieces.

$\frac{1}{4}$ means one quarter or one out of four equal pieces.

$\frac{2}{4}$ means two quarters or two out of four equal pieces.

$\frac{3}{4}$ means three quarters or three out of four equal pieces.

📄 Revise

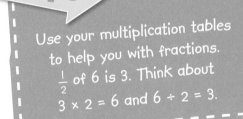

Tips

Use your multiplication tables to help you with fractions. $\frac{1}{2}$ of 6 is 3. Think about $3 \times 2 = 6$ and $6 \div 2 = 3$.

Here are 6 stars.

They are in two equal groups of 3.

So half of all the stars is 3.

We can write $\frac{1}{2}$ of 6 is 3.

Here is a stick.

This stick is 20cm long.

Half of the stick is 10cm long.

$\frac{1}{2}$ of 20cm = 10cm

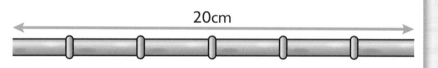

20cm

Use these stars to help you.

Count the stars.

How many groups of two stars can you make?

Yes, 4 groups.

So one group of two is $\frac{1}{4}$ of the stars.

$\frac{1}{4}$ of 8 is 2.

How many is $\frac{2}{4}$ of the stars?

How many is $\frac{3}{4}$ of the stars?

$\frac{2}{4}$ of 8 is 4.

$\frac{3}{4}$ of 8 is 6.

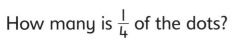 Talk maths

Here is an array of 12 dots.

Discuss the answers to these questions with a friend or adult.

How many is $\frac{1}{4}$ of the dots?

How many is $\frac{1}{3}$ of the dots?

How many is $\frac{3}{4}$ of the dots?

✔ Check

1. **You may find it helpful to draw some dots to help you to work out the answers.**

a. $\frac{1}{2}$ of 10 = ⬚

b. $\frac{2}{4}$ of 16 = ⬚

c. $\frac{1}{4}$ of 8 = ⬚

d. $\frac{3}{4}$ of 16 = ⬚

⚠ Problems

Brain-teaser Sandeep cuts off $\frac{1}{4}$ of a 24cm piece of tape.

Write a fraction number sentence to show how much Sandeep cut.

_____

Brain-buster Bella chooses a pencil that is 18cm long.
Her naughty brother keeps sharpening the pencil until there is 12cm left.

What fraction of the pencil has gone? ⬚

Recognising that $\frac{2}{4}$ is equivalent to $\frac{1}{2}$

↻ Recap

Look at this square.

It is divided into two equal parts.

So these are each worth half or $\frac{1}{2}$.

This square has been divided into quarters.

There are four quarters.

Each part is one quarter or $\frac{1}{4}$.

📋 Revise

half quarter

The two quarters and the half take up the same amount of room.

They are equal. So $\frac{2}{4} = \frac{1}{2}$.

This square has one side divided into quarters.

There are two quarters.

The other side is $\frac{1}{2}$.

$\frac{1}{4}$ of 12 is 3.

$\frac{2}{4}$ of 12 is 6.

$\frac{1}{2}$ of 12 is 6.

$\frac{2}{4}$ and $\frac{1}{2}$ are the same amount.

This rectangle is made from 12 squares.

This pencil is 16cm long. Can you work out:

$\frac{1}{4}$ of 16

$\frac{2}{4}$ of 16

$\frac{1}{2}$ of 16

16cm

What do you notice about $\frac{2}{4}$ and $\frac{1}{2}$?

4, 8, 8.
$\frac{2}{4}$ and $\frac{1}{2}$ are the same.

💡 Tips

If you split something in half the two pieces must be the same size. If you split something into quarters, each of the four pieces must be the same size.

💬 Talk maths

Work with a partner to draw different-sized rectangles and squares on squared paper and divide them into fractions. Try drawing some that have 20 small squares in them.

✔ Check

1. What is $\frac{1}{4}$ of 20? ☐   What is $\frac{2}{4}$ of 20? ☐

   So what is $\frac{1}{2}$ of 20? ☐

2. How much is $\frac{1}{4}$ of 8kg? ☐ kg   How much is $\frac{2}{4}$ of 8kg? ☐ kg

   So how much is $\frac{1}{2}$ of 8kg? ☐ kg

3. How much is $\frac{1}{4}$ of 24cm? ☐ cm   How much is $\frac{2}{4}$ of 24cm? ☐ cm

   So how much is $\frac{1}{2}$ of 24cm? ☐ cm

⚠ Problems

Brain-teaser Jonas has a small bag of gravel. It weighs 16kg.

How much does $\frac{1}{4}$ of the bag weigh? ☐ kg

So how much will $\frac{1}{2}$ of the bag weigh? ☐ kg

Brain-buster Jonas has a bucket of water with 12 litres in it.

He pours out $\frac{1}{4}$ of the water. Then he pours out another $\frac{1}{4}$ of the water.

What fraction of the water is left in the bucket? ☐

How many litres are left in the bucket? ☐

Comparing and ordering measurements

↻ Recap

We measure length using units.
This toy is 7cm tall.

📋 Revise

These are the short ways of writing units of measures.

centimetre ⟶ cm   kilogram ⟶ kg   gram ⟶ g

metre ⟶ m   millilitre ⟶ ml   litre ⟶ l

Measurements can be ordered and compared using <, > or =.

Decide which is longer.
30cm > 20cm

20cm

Decide which is lighter.
$1\frac{1}{2}$ kg < 3kg

Decide which container contains
more liquid. 5l > 2l

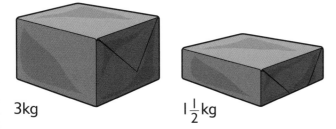

3kg $1\frac{1}{2}$ kg

5l

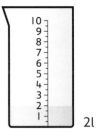
2l

Scale A shows weighing in grams.
The mass is 50g.

Scale B shows weighing in kilograms.
The mass is 2kg.

A

B

Tips 💡

Always make sure that
the measurements are
in the same unit.

🗨 *Talk maths*

Look at these three lengths.   50cm   90cm   40cm

Start with the units.

Are they all the same?

> Look at the tens numbers to find the largest. The order will be 90cm, 50cm and 40cm.

Discuss with a friend or adult how you could order them from shortest to longest.

Do this again with these weights.   500g   950g   600g

They are all in grams.

Here are some measurements in litres.

$\frac{1}{2}$ litre   3 litres $2\frac{1}{2}$ litres

> Look at the hundreds digit this time. The order is 500g, 600g and 950g.

✔ Check

1. **Write < or > to compare these measures to show which is larger.**

   a. 20km ☐ 25km

   b. $1\frac{1}{2}$ litres ☐ $\frac{1}{2}$ litre

2. **Now write these measures in order. Start with the smallest.**

   a. 55cm, 45cm, 48cm _____

   b. 6kg, 5kg, 4kg _____

   c. 3 litres, 4 litres, $3\frac{1}{2}$ litres _____

⚠ Problems

Brain-teaser Tania has a 30cm ruler. Sophy has a 25cm ruler.

Who has the longer ruler? _____

Brain-buster Tom and Katie are using sticky tape on a birthday gift. Tom uses 15cm of tape. Tania uses 17cm of tape.

Who uses more tape? _____

Cindy buys two bags of sweets that each weighs 40g. Sacha buys 60g of sweets.

Who has the heavier sweets? _____

Choosing and using standard units

↻ Recap

Mass is measured in kilograms and grams.

Capacity is measured in litres and millilitres.

Temperature is measured in degrees Celsius. We write °C.

Lengths are measured in metres and centimetres.

🗎 Revise

Before you measure something make an estimate and write it down. Use your eyes.

How long does something look?
How high is the water in the jug?
How much do you think that is?
Pick up the item to be weighed.
How heavy does it feel to you?

Look at these measuring tools.

The scale is marked in 100g from 0g to 1kg.
So it increases by 100g each time.

What mass does this show?

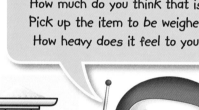

The scale is marked in 1cm.
So it increases by 1cm each time.

What length does the arrow show?

The scale is marked in 100ml.
So it increases by 100ml each time.

How much is in the jug?

600g, 15cm
500ml, 23°C

The scale is marked in 2°C. So it increases by 2°C each time. The little line in between marks the next 1°C.

What temperature is shown?

Tips 💡

Check the scale before making a reading.
Decide what the reading is halfway between each number.

50

💬 Talk maths

Look at the scales below.

Talk with a friend or an adult about the different scales.

What unit is shown on each scale?

Read each scale. What measurement does it show?

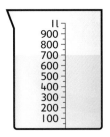

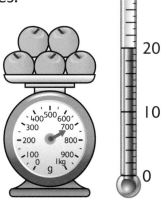

✔ Check

1. **Here are some measuring tools. Draw a line to show the measurement.**

   a. Draw an arrow at 13cm.

   b. Draw the hand to show 300g.

   c. Draw a line for 700ml.

   d. Draw an arrow at 17°C.

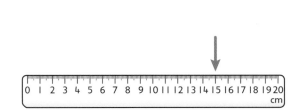
a

b

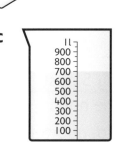
c

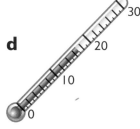
d

⚠ Problems

Brain-teaser This thermometer shows the morning temperature and the afternoon temperature.

How much warmer was it in the afternoon than in the morning? ☐ °C

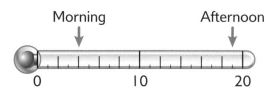
Morning   Afternoon
0   10   20

Brain-buster Marc weighed out the same amount of butter, flour and sugar. The scale shows how heavy the butter was.

What was the total weight of the butter, flour and sugar? ☐ g

Telling the time

↻ Recap

The short hand points to the hour.

The long hand points to how many minutes.

This clock shows 9 hours and 0 minutes.

The time is 9 o'clock.

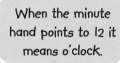

When the minute hand points to 12 it means o'clock.

目 Revise

Count the minutes in 5s.

Start at 12.

Count around the clock in 5s for the minutes.

You counted 60 minutes.

Up to 30 minutes we say 5 past, 10 past, quarter past, 20 past, 25 past the hour.

Then we say 25 to, 20 to, quarter to, 10 to and 5 to the next hour.

When the longer hand points to 6, that is 30 minutes past, or half past the hour.

💡 Tips

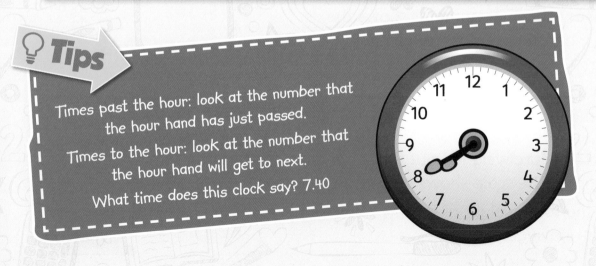

Times past the hour: look at the number that the hour hand has just passed.

Times to the hour: look at the number that the hour hand will get to next.

What time does this clock say? 7.40

💬 Talk maths

Look at this clock.

Talk with a partner.

Discuss what time you think this clock shows.

Can you explain why?

What time does this clock show?

How many minutes to 6 is it?

✔ Check

1. Draw the hands on the clock faces for these times.

a. Quarter past seven

b. Quarter to three

c. Five past two

d. Twenty past nine

⚠ Problems

Brain-teaser Jamie arrives at school at ten to nine. Draw the hands on the clock face to show this time.

Brain-buster These clocks show what time Jan leaves home and what time she arrives at the library.

How many minutes does her journey take?

_____

Leaves home

Arrives at library

53

Comparing and sequencing time

↺ Recap

Remember these facts.

There are 7 days in a week.

An hour has 60 minutes.

Revise

Count round the clock from 12 and back again in 5s.

You should count to 60. That is the number of minutes in an hour.

Look at these two clocks.

Clock A shows 5 o'clock.

Clock B shows 10 minutes past 5.

To work out the time difference between the two clocks count on in 5 minutes from 5 o'clock to 10 past 5.

This gives a count of 5, then 10.

So 10 minutes has passed.

A

B

Look at these two clocks.

Clock C shows 10 minutes past 3.

Clock D shows 20 minutes to 4.

To find the difference in time between the two clocks count on in minutes from the 10 minutes past to the 20 minutes to time.

C

D

This clock face shows the position of the two long hands shown on clocks C and D.

Count in 5s. 5, 10, 15, 20, 25, 30.

So the difference between the two times is 30 minutes.

💬 Talk maths

Clock E shows 20 minutes past 8.

How many minutes is it until 20 minutes to 9?

Clock F shows 10 minutes to 5.

How many minutes is it until quarter past 5?

10 minutes to 5 o'clock: 5, 10.

5 o'clock to quarter past 5: 15, 20, 25.

The time difference is 25 minutes.

Point with your finger and count in 5s.

✔ Check

1. **Which clock shows the earlier time?**

2. **Which clock shows the later time?**

3. **Which clock shows a half past time?**

4. **Which clock shows a quarter to time?**

5. **How many minutes are there from the clock G time to the clock H time?** _____ minutes

⚠ Problems

Brain-teaser Mark leaves for school at half past eight.

He gets to school at 5 minutes to 9.

How long does it take Mark to get to school? _____ minutes

Brain-buster Ellie does her maths homework from five past four to half past four. She then does her English homework from half past four until ten to five.

Which homework takes longer? _____

How many minutes longer? _____ minutes

Money

↻ Recap

Here are the coins we use.

Make sure you can recognise each coin and name it.

🗒 Revise

Different ways of making 50p.

 This is a 50p coin.

20p + 20p + 10p makes 50p.

Use coins to help you to find the total.

This is another way to make 50p.

Tips 💡

To write an amount of money less than £1, write the p sign after the price, like this.

To write an amount of money in pounds, the £ sign goes before the price, like this.

£1

£2

When finding the cost of two items begin by adding the tens then the ones. Try this.

21p + 32p = 20p + 30p + 1p + 2p = 50p + 3p = 53p

🗩 Talk maths

Talk with a partner about the easiest way to add these coins.

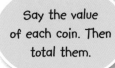
Say the value of each coin. Then total them.

Always start with the largest value and end with the smallest... so 10p add 5p add 2p is 17p.

£2 and £1 is £3. Then add the pence coins. £3 add 50p add 20p is £3 and 70p.

50p add 10p is 60p. Then add the smallest value coin. 60p add 5p is 65p

✔ Check

1. **Write a coin number sentence that totals 15p.**

   _____

2. **Which coins could you use to make a total of 22p?**

   _____

3. **Write a coin number sentence that totals 45p.**

   _____

⚠ Problems

Brain-teaser Lara buys a key ring for 75p. Write a coin number sentence to total 75p. Use as few coins as possible.

_____

Brain-buster Find three different ways of making £1 using coins.
Write a number sentence for each one.

_____

_____

_____

Solving money problems

Recap

There are 100p in £1.

Revise

Tom spends 13p. How much change does he get from 20p?

You decide which method you like.

There are two ways to solve this.

Count up from 13 to 20 as if you are giving change:

13 to 15 is 2.

Then 15 to 20 is 5. So that is 2 + 5 is 7. The change is 7p.

Or take 13 away from 20 by counting back.

Now try these.

Tom buys a pen for 12p and a notebook for 5p.
How much change will he have from 20p?

12p and 5p is 17p. Counting up to 20p is another 3p. So Tom has 3p change.

Sarah buys a comic for 32p and a pen for 16p.
How much change does she have from 50p?

One way to do this is to add 10p then 6p. So 32p add 10p is 42p and add 6p is 48p. So Sarah gets 2p change.

You can write this out as an addition sentence like this.

$32 + 16 = 32 + 10 + 6 = 42 + 6 = 48$

$50 - 48 = 2.$

So the change is 2p.

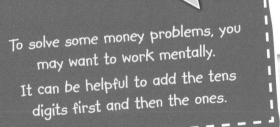

Tips

To solve some money problems, you may want to work mentally.
It can be helpful to add the tens digits first and then the ones.

💬 Talk maths

Count up to work out the change with a friend or an adult.

16p →

13p →

37p →

```
0  1  2  3  4  5  6  7  8  9  10  11  12  13  14  15  16  17  18  19  20
```

✔ Check

1. **Write the total.**

   a.   23p + 16p = ☐ p

   b.   38p + 19p = ☐ p

2. **Write the change.**

   a.   20p − 16p = ☐ p

   b.   50p − 29p = ☐ p

⚠ Problems

Brain-teaser Pip spends 3p on a chew and 9p on a lolly.

How much change does Pip receive from 20p? ☐ p

Brain-buster Mina buys two notepads at 24p each and a pen for 47p.

How much change does Mina receive from £1? ☐ p

Comparing and sorting 2D shapes

These are 2D shapes. That means they are flat, like a picture in a book.

↺ Recap

 circle

 triangle

 square

rectangle

 hexagon

 pentagon

octagon

semicircle

A corner on a shape is called a **vertex**. Two or more are called **vertices**.

📄 Revise

	Number of sides	**Number of vertices**
Triangle	3	3
Square	4	4
Rectangle	4	4
Pentagon	5	5
Hexagon	6	6
Octagon	8	8

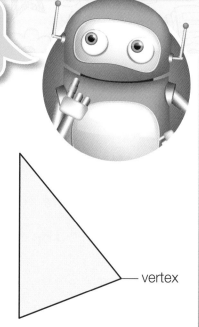

— vertex

What do you notice about the number of sides and the number of vertices? For these shapes, these numbers are the same.

The circle is different. It has one side and no vertices.

Some shapes have a line of symmetry. Look at these.

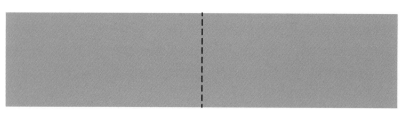

This rectangle has a line of symmetry.
One side of the line is a mirror image of the other.

Tips

If you need help with symmetry, use a mirror to check.
Put the mirror on the line.
Look in the mirror.
What can you see?

💬 Talk maths

Let's look at this triangle.

The line goes through the middle of the triangle.

What you see one side of the line is a mirror image of what is on the other side of the line.

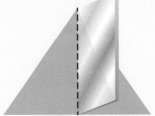

If you are not sure whether there is a line of symmetry, draw the shape carefully onto some paper. Cut it out. Now try folding to see if you can find a line of symmetry.

Another way is to use a mirror like this.

Look in the mirror.

If what you see is the rest of the shape then you have found a line of symmetry.

How would you explain to someone how to find out whether there is a line of symmetry for the rectangle?

✔ Check

1. **How many sides does a pentagon have?**

2. **How many vertices does an octagon have?**

3. **Which shapes have curved sides?** _____

⚠ Problems

Brain-teaser This is a hexagon. Draw a line of symmetry.

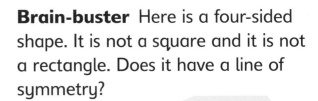

Brain-buster Here is a four-sided shape. It is not a square and it is not a rectangle. Does it have a line of symmetry?

_____

Comparing and sorting 3D shapes

↻ Recap

These are 3D shapes. That means they are solid.

 cone

 cylinder

 triangular prism

 pyramid (square based)

 sphere

 pentagonal prism

 cube

 cuboid

📄 Revise

A face is a side of a 3D shape.

An edge is the line where two faces meet.

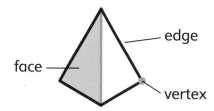

edge

face

vertex

A vertex is where two straight edges meet. Two or more are called vertices.

Look at these shapes.

Think about the parts of the shapes that are hidden in the pictures.

How many vertices, faces and edges does each shape have?
We can write these into the table.

Shape	Number of vertices	Number of faces	Number of edges
Cone	0	2	1
Cylinder	0	3	2
Triangular prism	6	5	9
Square-based pyramid	5	5	8

Tips 💡

In a picture you cannot see all of the 3D shape.

Find an object that you can pick up if you are stuck.

For example, a cereal pack is a cuboid, and a can of beans is a cylinder.

💬 Talk maths

Look around you at school and at home.
What 3D shapes can you find?

A shoe box is a good example of a cuboid.
You may find a cylinder in the food cupboard.
It could be a tin of food or a packet of biscuits.

Can you find anything that is cone shaped?
Perhaps you have some building bricks that
you could use?

Discuss each shape that you find.
How many faces, vertices and edges does
each shape have?

> I counted
> 6 faces, 8 vertices
> and 12 edges.

✔ Check

1. Use the shape pictures to help you to answer these questions.

a. Which shapes have curved faces? _____

b. Which shape has the most edges? _____

c. How many vertices does the cone have? ☐

⚠ Problems

Brain-teaser Myla says that the two 3D shapes she chose have five faces in total. Which two shapes do you think she chose?

_____

Brain-buster Mark has a shape that has five faces and another shape with 9 edges. Which two shapes do you think he chose?

_____

Recognising 2D shapes on the surface of 3D shapes

↻ Recap

Here are some 3D shapes.

Look at the different shapes that can be seen on these shapes.

Look for circles, squares and triangles.

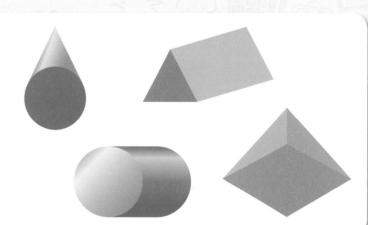

📄 Revise

The flat faces are 2D shapes.

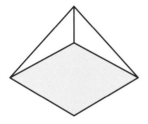

pyramid

cuboid

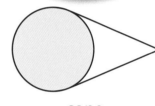

cone

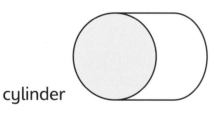

cylinder

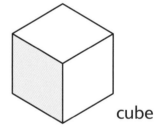

cube

3D shapes have faces that can be curved or flat.

Look at the pyramid.

It has a square for its base and a triangle for the other faces.

Now look at the cylinder. It has a circle face at each end.

Its other face is curved.

The cone has a circle for its base.

Its other face curves up to a point which is the apex.

The cube has six square faces.

Each face is exactly the same as the other five.

The cuboid has rectangles as some of its faces.

Some 3D shapes have opposite faces that are all the same.

 Talk maths

Work with a friend or adult.

Discuss the 3D shapes that you know.

Can you think of an example of a 3D shape that has only square faces?

Which shapes have rectangles on some faces?

✔ Check

1. **Think about things around you.**

   a. Name something that has a circle for a face.

   _____

   b. Name something that has a rectangle for a face.

   _____

   c. Name something that has a triangle for a face.

   _____

⚠ Problems

Brain-teaser Steve builds a model with some building bricks. He chooses some shapes with two circle faces. He chooses other shapes with three rectangle faces and two triangle faces.

Which shapes did he choose? _____ and _____

Brain-buster Sally builds a model too. She chooses shapes that have two triangle faces but five faces altogether. She chooses some more shapes with one square face. She also chooses some shapes that have just one circle face.

Which shapes does she choose? _____ , _____

and _____

Patterns and sequences

↺ Recap

Look around you.

Is there wallpaper on the wall?
Does it have a pattern?

Look at this piece of wallpaper.

This is a repeating pattern.

📋 Revise

A repeating pattern like this has the same items in the same order. This is repeated each time.

Look carefully at this arrangement.

It is a repeating pattern. The pattern is triangle rectangle rectangle.
That pattern repeats.

Say this pattern.
The pattern is: square triangle circle.
This pattern can repeat again and again.

Tips 💡

Saying the pattern aloud helps you to see that it repeats.

💬 Talk maths

Say these pattern beginnings.
Say what comes next.

✔ Check

1. **Continue the pattern for two repeats.**

2. **Continue this pattern for two repeats.**

3. **Look carefully at these patterns. ✔ them if they repeat correctly. Put a ✘ if not correct.**

a.

b.

c.

⚠ Problems

Brain-teaser John makes this pattern. Draw the next four shapes in the pattern.

Brain-buster Jenny draws this pattern. What is missing?

Position, direction and movement

↻ Recap

If Jo makes a quarter turn, she will face the car.

If she makes a half turn, she will face the book.

If she makes a three-quarter turn, she will face the drum.

If she makes a whole turn, she will face the teddy.

📄 Revise

 Look at the two clocks. On the second clock the minute hand has turned through a right angle. A right angle is a quarter turn.

 The minute hand of a clock moves to make a half turn, or two right angles.

 And the hand turns through another right angle to show a three-quarter turn.

 When the clock shows 10 o'clock the minute hand has turned through 4 right angles. It has made a full turn.

Now look at these two pictures.

Sam has walked along the road in a straight line.

✔ Check

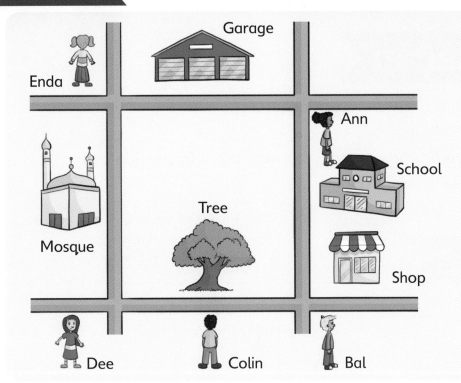

1. **Ann turns a right angle to the right. What will she see?**

   _____

2. **Bal turns a right angle anticlockwise. What will he see?**

   _____

3. **Colin crosses the road and walks straight ahead. What will he see?**

   _____

4. **Dee turns two right angles clockwise. What will she see?**

   _____

5. **Enda turns anticlockwise through three right angles. What will she see?**

   _____

⚠ Problems

Brain-teaser On a separate piece of paper, draw the route James takes to school. He leaves his house and turns left one right angle. He walks along the road to the crossroads. He turns left again. His school is there.

Interpreting and making simple data charts

↺ Recap

Sometimes we collect information about things like favourite colour, pets, holidays.

We need to have a way to show the information so that it is easy to read and understand.

> All these charts show the same information about the children's favourite colours.

> There are 7 blue tallies.

目 Revise

Tally chart

Colour	Tally
Blue	卌 II
Red	卌 卌 III
Yellow	卌 I

Tallies are a quick way to collect the information.

Look at the blue row.

It has |||| to show 4, and then a line through for 5.

Count the tallies for each colour.

Table

This table contains numbers instead of tallies.

Compare it with the tally chart.

You should find the same information.

Colour	Number of children
Blue	7
Red	13
Yellow	6

Pictogram

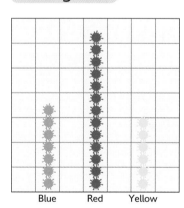

Blue   Red   Yellow

On the pictogram.

One ✳ stands for one vote for a colour.

Count the pictures for blue, red and yellow.

Are these the same as in the tally chart? They should be!

Block chart

The block graph has a scale that goes up in 2s on the left-hand side.

Compare the table and the block graph.

They show the same information!

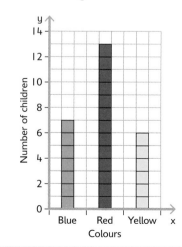

💬 Talk maths

Look at the graphs and tables on page 70.

Talk about how they are the same and how they are different.

Which do you think is the best one for showing favourite colours?

✔ Check

Some children collected this information. Write it in the table.

Title:

Dogs	
Cats	
Rabbits	
Mice	

1. 卌 ||| children have cats as pets.

2. 卌 卌 || children have dogs as pets.

3. 卌 || children have rabbits as pets.

4. |||| children have mice as pets.

5. Write a title for your table.

6. Draw a pictogram or block graph for the data.

⚠ Problems

Brain-teaser Five more children buy mice. Which pet is least popular now?

_____

Brain-buster How many more children like cats and dogs than like rabbits?

71

Using and making charts

↺ Recap

Graphs show you information with pictures, blocks, tallies or numbers.

📋 Revise

Look at the block graph.

Count the wins for Monday. How many games did Tom win on the other days?

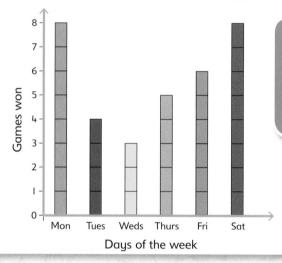

Tom plays an online game against his friend. The block graph shows the numbers of times he won the game each day.

✔ Check

1. On which day did Tom win six games? _____

2. How many games did Tom win on Wednesday? ☐

3. When did Tom win four games? _____

4. What was the score for Thursday? ☐

5. On which two days did Tom win the same number of games?

_____

⚠ Problems

Brain-teaser Tom forgot that he had won another game on Wednesday. Add this to the block graph. How many games did he win on Wednesday? ☐

Making totals and comparisons

↺ Recap

You can find information from a chart or diagram.

▤ Revise

This block graph shows the colours of shoes worn by a class of children.
The scale at the side goes up in 2s.
Count the blocks for each colour.

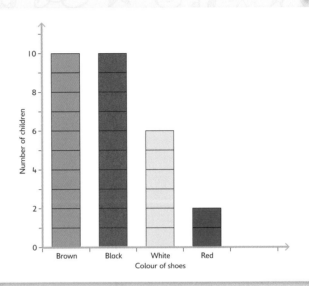

✔ Check

Use the block diagram to answer the questions.

1. **Which two colours scored the same number?**

   _____ and _____

2. **How many pairs of shoes are there in total?** ⬜

3. **Five more children came into the classroom. They all wore blue shoes. Make a column on the block diagram for the blue shoes.**

4. **How many more children wore black shoes than blue shoes?** ⬜

⚠ Problems

Brain-buster Which is more? The number of children wearing black shoes and red shoes, or the number of children wearing brown shoes and white shoes?

_____ and _____ How many more? ⬜

Answers: Year 2

NUMBER AND PLACE VALUE

Page 9

1   **a.** 14, 12, 10   **b.** 12, 9, 6

2   **a.** 50, 60, 70   **b.** 20, 15, 10

3   4, 14, 24, 34, 44, 54, 64, 74, 84, 94

Brain-teaser: 18
Brain-buster: 10

Page 11

1   **a.** 53   **b.** 99   **c.** 6   **d.** 34   **e.** 22   **f.** 100

2   **a.** eighty-one   **b.** fourteen   **c.** sixty-two   **d.** thirty-eight
    e. ninety   **f.** forty-seven

Brain-teaser: **a.** ✗ **b.** ✓ **c.** ✓ **d.** ✗
Brain-buster: fifty-eight

Page 13

1   **a.** <   **b.** =   **c.** >   **d.** 5

2   37, 59, 64, 72, 91

Brain-teaser: Jamie
Brain-buster: Any number between 44 and 49

Page 15

1   47

2   Check that there are five beads on the 10s and one bead on
    the 1s

3   6 in 61 is the largest 10s digit
    1 in 61 is the smallest 1s digit

Brain-teaser: 7
Brain-buster: 87

Page 17

1   Check that the position of 43 is a reasonable estimate.

2   **a.** 35   **b.** 58   **c.** 83

Brain-teaser: Check that the position of 42 is a reasonable
estimate.

Page 19

1   **a.** 10   **b.** 50   **c.** 80   **d.** 40   **e.** 70   **f.** 50

Brain-teaser: 30
Brain-buster: 20

ADDITION AND SUBTRACTION

Page 21

1   **a.** 18 and 28   **b.** 2 and 22   **c.** 15 and 35   **d.** 9 and 29

    e. 19 and 39

Brain-teaser: 26
Brain-buster: 21

Page 23

1   **a.** 49   **b.** 95   **c.** 41   **d.** 91   **e.** 59   **f.** 62

Brain-teaser: 44
Brain-buster: 32

Page 25

1   **a.** 71   **b.** 89   **c.** 65   **d.** 35   **e.** 68   **f.** 28

Brain-teaser: 18
Brain-buster: 51

Page 27

1   **a.** 8   **b.** 12

2   **a.** 20   **b.** 19   **c.** 16

Brain-teaser: 18
Brain-buster: 20

Page 29

1   19 − 7 = 12   ✓

2   29 − 9 = 20   ✗

3   31 + 4 = 35   ✓

4   27 − 13 = 14   ✗

5   31 + 23 = 54   ✓

Brain-teaser: 32 + 32 = 64; 64 − 32 = 32
Brain-buster: 35 + 24 = 59. 59 − 4 = 55; 55 + 4 = 59

Page 31

1   46

2   29

Brain-teaser: 60p

MULTIPLICATION AND DIVISION

Page 33

1   **a.** 60   **b.** 30   **c.** 100   **d.** 5   **e.** 9

Brain-teaser: 40
Brain-buster: 40

Page 35

1   **a.** 5 × 7 = 35 or 7 × 5 = 35
    b. 5 × 10 = 50 or 10 × 5 = 50
    c. 2 × 8 = 16 or 8 × 2 = 16
    d. 12 × 2 = 24 or 2 × 12 = 24

2   **a.** 6 ÷ 2 = 3   **b.** 25 ÷ 5 = 5

Brain-teaser: 40
Brain-buster: 6

1 92, 80

2 83, 7

3 even

4 odd

5 even

Brain-teaser: 73
Brain-buster: odd

Page 39

1 **a.** Array of 5 rows by 2 **b.** Array of 6 rows by 5
   c. Array of 2 rows by 10

2 **a.** $7 \times 2 = 14$; $2 \times 7 = 14$; $14 \div 2 = 7$; $14 \div 7 = 2$
   b. $4 \times 5 = 20$; $5 \times 4 = 20$; $20 \div 4 = 5$; $20 \div 5 = 4$
   c. $3 \times 10 = 30$; $10 \times 3 = 30$; $30 \div 3 = 10$; $30 \div 10 = 3$

Brain-teaser: $6 \times 2 = 12$; $2 \times 6 = 12$

Brain-buster: 30

Page 40

1 **a.** ✓ **b.** ✗ **c.** ✓ **d.** ✗ **e.** ✓

Brain-teaser: Answer is correct. £1 is 100p. A check calculation is $64p + 36p = 100p$.

Page 41

1 **a.** $5 \times 2 = 10$; $2 \times 5 = 10$
   b. $5 \times 10 = 50$; $10 \times 5 = 50$
   c. $2 \times 3 = 6$; $3 \times 2 = 6$
   d. $5 \times 8 = 40$; $8 \times 5 = 40$

Brain-teaser: Correct. Because $3 \times 5 = 15$ or $5 \times 3 = 15$.

FRACTIONS

Page 43

1 **a.** $\frac{1}{3}$ **b.** $\frac{3}{4}$ **c.** $\frac{2}{4}$ or $\frac{1}{2}$ **d.** $\frac{2}{4}$ or $\frac{1}{2}$

Brain-teaser: $\frac{2}{4}$ or $\frac{1}{2}$

Brain-buster: $\frac{1}{4}$

Page 45

1 **a.** 5 **b.** 8 **c.** 2 **d.** 12

Brain-teaser: $\frac{1}{4}$ of 24cm = 6cm

Brain-buster: $\frac{1}{3}$

Page 47

1 5, 10, 10

2 2kg, 4kg, 4kg

3 6cm, 12cm, 12cm

Brain-teaser: 4kg, 8kg

Brain-buster: $\frac{1}{2}$ or $\frac{2}{4}$; 6 litres

MEASUREMENT

Page 49

1 **a.** < **b.** >

2 **a.** 45cm, 48cm, 55cm **b.** 4kg, 5kg, 6kg **c.** 3 litres, $3\frac{1}{2}$ litres, 4 litres

Brain-teaser: Tania
Brain-buster: Katie; Cindy

Page 51

1 **a.** Check the measurement shows 13cm on ruler.
   b. Check the measurement shows 300g on the scales.
   c. Check the measurement shows 700ml on the jug.
   d. Check the measurement shows 17°C on the thermometer.

Brain-teaser: 15°C
Brain-buster: 450g

Page 53

Check that the hour hand and minute hand are correctly positioned for:

1 **a.** Quarter past seven **b.** Quarter to three **c.** Five past two **d.** Twenty past nine

Brain-teaser: Check that the hands are correctly drawn for 8.50.
Brain-buster: 20 minutes

Page 55

1 G

2 H

3 G

4 H

5 15 minutes

Brain-teaser: 25 minutes
Brain-buster: maths; 5 minutes

Page 57

1 Coin total of 15p, such as $10p + 5p = 15p$

2 Coin total of 22p, such as $20p + 2p = 22p$

3 Coin total of 45p, such as $20p + 20p + 5p = 45p$

Brain-teaser: $50p + 20p + 5p = 75p$
Brain-buster: Total of £1 each time, e.g. $50p + 50p = £1$; $20p + 20p + 10p + 50p = £1$; $20p + 20p + 20p + 20p + 20p = £1$

Page 59

1 **a.** 39p **b.** 57p

2 **a.** 4p **b.** 21p

Brain-teaser: 8p
Brain-buster: 5p

GEOMETRY

Page 61

1 5

2 8

3 circle, semicircle

Brain-teaser: Check that the line of symmetry has been drawn correctly either from one vertex to the opposite vertex or from the middle of a side to the middle of the opposite side.
Brain-buster: No, this is an irregular quadrilateral with no lines of symmetry.

Page 63

1 **a.** sphere, cylinder, cone **b.** triangular prism **c.** 0

Brain-teaser: cone and cylinder
Brain-buster: square-based pyramid and triangular prism

Page 65

1 **a.** For example, a clock **b.** For example, a microwave oven or television **c.** For example, a chocolate box.

Brain-teaser: cylinders and triangular prisms
Brain-buster: triangular prisms, square-based pyramids and cones

Page 67

1 Check that children have drawn pattern correctly (circle, circle, square, triangle).

2 Check that children have drawn pattern correctly (triangle, circle, star, star, star).

3 **a.** ✓ **b.** ✗ **c.** ✗

Brain-teaser: Check that children have drawn pattern correctly (circle, diamond, diamond, diamond).
Brain-buster: In the pattern, there are two circles and then a triangle at the end of the pattern. One circle is missing.

Page 69

1 School

2 Shop

3 Tree

4 Mosque

5 Garage

Brain-teaser: Check that the route is correct.

STATISTICS

Page 71

1–4

Cats	Dogs	Rabbits	Mice
8	12	7	4

5 Title: for example, Our pets

6 Check the pictogram or block graph match the data.

Brain-teaser: Rabbit
Brain-buster: 13

Page 72

1 Friday

2 3

3 Tuesday

4 5

5 Monday and Saturday

Brain-teaser: 4

Page 73

1 Black and brown

2 28

3 Additional column of 5 blocks. Label to read Blue

4 5

Brain-buster: Brown and white. 4 more.

Glossary

< Less than
12 < 13 means 12 is less than 13.

> Greater than
13 > 12 means 13 is greater than 12.

2D shapes These are flat shapes such as these.

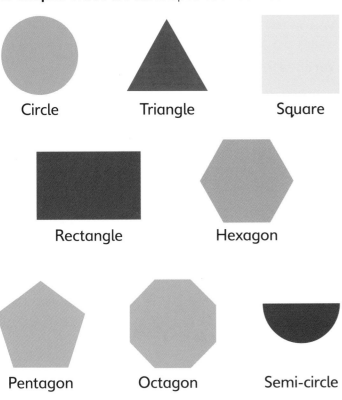

Circle   Triangle   Square

Rectangle   Hexagon

Pentagon   Octagon   Semi-circle

3D shapes These are solid shapes such as these.

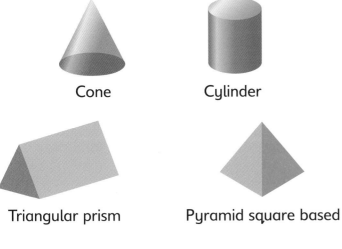

Cone   Cylinder

Triangular prism   Pyramid square based

Sphere   Cube   Cuboid

A

Array A way of showing multiplication and division.

$$5 \times 3 = 15$$
$$3 \times 5 = 15$$
$$15 \div 3 = 5$$
$$15 \div 5 = 3$$

C

Calculation Working out the answer to any number sentence.

Commutative law The order in which addition or multiplication is calculated will not affect the answer. So addition and multiplication are commutative. Subtraction and division are not commutative.
So, $5 + 3 = 3 + 5$ but $5 - 3 \neq 3 - 5$. And $5 \times 3 = 3 \times 5$ but $15 \div 3 \neq 3 \div 15$.

D

Data charts These show information in different ways. For example, tally charts, pictograms, block charts.

Digit A single numeral such as 1, 5…9.

Division Repeated subtraction. So $15 - 5 - 5 - 5 = 0$. Or $15 \div 3 = 5$.

E

Edge An edge is where two faces of a solid shape meet. At either end of an edge there will be a vertex.

Equivalent Worth the same, for example $\frac{1}{2}$ is equivalent to $\frac{2}{4}$.

F

Face A flat or curved surface on a 3D shape.

Fortnight 2 weeks or 14 days.

Fraction A fraction is a part of a number, shape or measure that has been divided equally. For example, when a cake is cut into four equal slices, then one slice is $\frac{1}{4}$ of the cake.

M

Multiple A number that can be divided by another number exactly. For example, for 35, $7 \times 5 = 35$. So 35 is a multiple of 7 and 5.

Multiplication Repeated addition, for example, $5 + 5 + 5 = 15$ and $5 \times 3 = 15$.

O

Ones digit The digit in a number that shows how many ones there are. For example, in 25, the ones digit is the 5, for 5 ones.

R

Right angle Here is a right angle in a square.

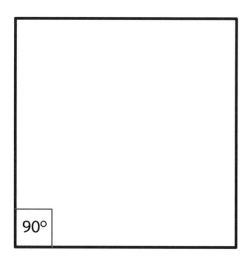

90°

Objects can make right-angle turns.

S

Standard units Metric units such as metres, centimetres, grams, kilograms, millilitres, litres, are standard units of measure. Imperial units such as ounces, pounds, yards, feet, inches, pints and gallons are also standard units.

T

Tens digit The tens digit is the digit in a number with two digits or more, which shows how many tens there are. For example: in 25, the 10s digit is the 2, for 2 tens.

V

Vertex The 'point' or 'corner' on a 2D or 3D shape where two straight lines meet.

Vertices Plural of 'vertex'.

Notes

Multiplication table

x	1	2	3	4	5	6	7	8	9	10	11	12
1	1	2	3	4	5	6	7	8	9	10	11	12
2	2	4	6	8	10	12	14	16	18	20	22	24
3	3	6	9	12	15	18	21	24	27	30	33	36
4	4	8	12	16	20	24	28	32	36	40	44	48
5	5	10	15	20	25	30	35	40	45	50	55	60
6	6	12	18	24	30	36	42	48	54	60	66	72
7	7	14	21	28	35	42	49	56	63	70	77	84
8	8	16	24	32	40	48	56	64	72	80	88	96
9	9	18	27	36	45	54	63	72	81	90	99	108
10	10	20	30	40	50	60	70	80	90	100	110	120
11	11	22	33	44	55	66	77	88	99	110	121	132
12	12	24	36	48	60	72	84	96	108	120	132	144